Orchestra of Stones

The Lapidary Songs

Orchestra of Stones

The Lapidary Songs

Poems By

W.C. Crutchfield Jr.

Spyglass Press

Eugene, OR

Acknowledgments:

The author gratefully acknowledges Pat Edwards and the staff at Groundwaters Publishing where some of these poems first appeared. My sincere thanks for their support and encouragement.

As well, a nod to David Daniel.
Your support, my friend, was invaluable.

I also thank my wife Mari.
Your patience, diligence and understanding made all this possible.

Cover art: Rocks, Pebbles, Sea
Photo by Robert Armstrong from Pixabay

W.C. Crutchfield Jr/Spyglass Press
1335 Hammock
Eugene, OR/97401

Publisher's Note: This is a work of fiction. Names, characters, places, and incidents are a product of the author's imagination. Locales and public names are sometimes used for atmospheric purposes. Any resemblance to actual people, living or dead, or to businesses, companies, events, institutions, or locales is completely coincidental.

Book Layout © 2017 BookDesignTemplates.com
Orchestra of Stones-The Lapidary Songs/
W. C. Crutchfield Jr. -- 1st ed.
ISBN:978-0-9843362-0-3

For Mari

the earth reveals itself in stones

the heart reveals itself in song

Contents

"I have seen a medicine
That's able to breathe life into a stone,
Quicken a rock, and make you dance canary
With spritely fire and motion"

Wm. Shakespeare — All's Well That Ends Well

Orchestra of Stones

The Lapidary Songs

quiet ocean

in the damp salt air of morning
a strange silent ocean is revealed,
the horizon expands, stretching out
beyond our vision, towards
the earth's simple inspiring curve

strangely quiet and composed, the water
    seems still,
collecting its' energy, patiently
awaiting the signal to approach the shore

ancient swells building, welling up
    in majestic volume
breaking free, cresting into waves of foam
    with a gentle fury
meeting their steady resolve

gravity's blue mirror seduces jagged peaks and
    headlands,
ravaging frigid glaciers and the fragile dunes
with constant scouring, surface and
core, washing away the mouths of rivers,

cleansing,
rinsing,
returning

strong steady pulse,
water in motion, measuring
rise and fall of inlets
and bays, their basins
filled and emptied,
tidal flow balancing the earth
to its heart,
returning
to its quiet ocean.

remembering small things

peculiar, those little moments we remember,
empty streets of childhood dawn,
the gentle warmth of morning asphalt
rising like sun through the clouds

the cool glistening green of canal banks,
cattails and rushes bending slightly in faint
    graceful breeze
dry cracked bark of locust and ash trees
    casting dust
amid the arid valley's skeletal bones,

why do these pictures stand out despite
the passage of time?
why do these small things loom
suddenly so large?

they resist forgetting, surviving in
the fact of their smallness, defiant in
the quiet corner of repose
graceful in the comfort of memory,
hardy survivors.

my place

it is early morning
dark with silence,
except for the whisper
of constellations above.
and walking out the door
coffee in hand,
books and binders
tucked under my arm
I sense that in this moment,
in these first few steps,
this is my simple little place
in the vast expanse of the world.
earth and sky connected
by feet on the ground
and step by step,
I move into my
place for the day

sliver of moon

who will remember
those forgotten moments,
passing so swiftly
memory can barely capture,
let alone preserve

there must be a way to insure
them from harm, to hold them close
to our hearts, safe from decay,
their legacy slipping away,
lost into the shadow of dreams,
like fading impressions of ink

trailing off like vapor, thin clouds against
the brilliance of blue sky
vanishing into just a trace,
a sliver of the moon

forgotten letters

the forgotten voices are calling,
letters from long ago,
torn from whispers and
enfolded in flowers

aroma of fresh fields swirling
in the locks of your hair,
and the salt of tears staining
these abandoned pages, turning
the pale ink into faded tattoos

the sad alphabet of distance still lingers,
flashing like birds against the cusp of twilight,
turning as one, weightless
against the empty air.

two stones

walking the stream's edge
the faint rhapsody of dawn
caressed the two stones
resting there in the quiet gravel

lying among the muted rust
and grey of many others,
they seemed to sparkle
as if prompting me to pocket them
daring me to favor one
or two above the rest

on the grey banks I paused
and considered them, marveling
at their residence here, the melody
of just two among the many,
imagining their long and patient journey

listening close I bent to hear
a song shared from an ancient past
the echoes of fire and ice transformed
through their patient and ageless hibernation

a chorus of rock ground away from massive
    slabs of earth,

cut and chiseled into separate notes
basalt and granite, charting this landscape
    anew,
scattered into a masterpiece of fragments
all the rough edges worn smooth and golden,
serenaded by the currents, kissed by winds,
scattered here before us like precious jewels
set into a small bezel of the world.

for now I must let them rest here
secure in this patient setting,
a slow measure of earth

the passage of days will take them up
as they will, in their measure of time,
returning them to dust,
and the orchestra of stones.

heartbreak

though I am no singer,
often I can hear these melodies
lingering in the stillness,
descending chords cascading,
full of resonant notes
flowing inside me,

full to bursting,
lungs overflowing with sweet response,
like breath drawn deep

the diastole of repose, a reprieve from
customary measures
and then the chest tightens
songs welling up inside, a silent heaviness
dissolved by the taste of salt on my cheek
the music slowly fading away

were you there

where you there
the other day
when I called

I heard the recorded voice,
it intoned the vague, familiar,
scheme—so false and
insincere

I imagined you there
lingering close by

tracing the urgency of
my concern

perhaps you were just in the other room
footsteps away, barely
out of reach

or far off
in another country
altogether

a landscape of dark shapes,
surrounding you

shadows swirling
shifting along the sands

echoes of pain and
mistrust--tide-swept
against the grain

a separate zone
from where you now
reside

did you hear the call
perhaps the ring startled you
from yesterday's sleep

or worse
has this insistent
ringing

pushed you closer,
towards today

two trees

late in the fall
during one of the warmer days
after the dark news had arrived
the grim diagnosis and the path unclear,
before the burning and chemicals
and the cutting began

we drove along the river
up towards a nursery set upon a hill
we brought home two trees
a dappled willow and the elegant
red bark maple

still in bloom for what
was left of the season

we set them in ceramic pots
their temporary homes, unsure of
where to plant them, how
to settle the earth around the roots,
fearful of the harsh winter coming

soon the trunks were bare,
still and dormant as the frozen light
and the days grew precious and short

with no choice we held our breath
waiting for the warmth of the sun
praying for the signs of life
watching through the frost
and listening for the thawing ice

dreaming of an early spring
when the strong sap would flow,
defying the cold hard earth
the buds bursting once again, veins filled
and pulsing with sweet nectar

roots finally taking hold
claiming a place in the ground,
beautiful anchors in this world

drawing a rune

on difficult days, in sudden moments
unplanned and unpredictable, I pull a stone
from the plain grey bag,

so random and unbidden, drawn
from its secure nest of darkness,
its silent warm cocoon.
placing it face down
I lightly touch the stones smooth surface,
caressing the tender white skin of the future,

a simple act, reaching out
to untie the drawstring, breath suspended
as the same tile spills out again,

the voice of Laguz whispers to me
of the mysteries of flowing water,
the force of moon's shadow,
the balance of gravity
pulling at some essential nature,

drawing me back inside,
back into the tides, plying the currents
of ancient oracles
drawing a rune.

up from below

a morning drive, not far by the standard of
    today
but far enough to give the sense of distance
    and remove
just enough to give a glimpse of the unfolding
    day

the morning commute bends traffic
    through the curves
slowing to a crawl across the green girded
    bridge
the view both east and west a stream of
    blue water, sparkling
in the panoramic softness of dawn's solitude,

stopping here a moment, maybe longer,
as the line of cars unwind

I am reassured of the day's promise,
soothed by the calm waters
lapping the river's edge
gently lined with weeping trees, rushes and
    deep pools.

longing to linger -above this placid
    expanse

the traffic melts away,
only the morning shadows creeping up
across the bridgework skeleton
gives a hint of time

then hours later, a day's work fulfilled
back across the water again, heat of the day
     rising
a harsh glare, shimmering off the surface

and out beyond the bridge, beyond the
     creaking green steel
floats a festival of color, the orange and yellow
     hues
tubes and rafts dot the water,
mayflies skimming the surface

the parents with children,
the friends and the lovers
all carefree,
dipping into the cool water

floating out under the bridge, laughing and
     smiling
waving up towards the traffic
moving slowly back home

tempting me to join them,
shouting from below
"come on in,
     the water's fine!"

the taste of ashes

I remember this particular spot,
out in front of the ancient stone bench
perched above the tide pools and chasms
below, under a fearless totem
defiant and set out on the edge of the sea

the curve and curl of water below spits out the
    waves
in a wash of foam, rolling in and out, surge
    and pause
retreating to gather more strength,
    drawn back into its own vastness
collecting the salt and spray
filling our lungs to bursting, with a
    strange sweetness
swallowing the sea's furious energy, making it
    our own.

"this is the spot," you said, "right here,"
on the bluff where the horizon expands,
where the wind-blown reeds and beach grass
reach up, defying the dunes,
touching the tideline of stars, caressing
the mysterious light of midnight heavens,
where the constellations swirl forever,

frozen nebulae spinning away at such speeds
   we cannot fathom.

I taste a peculiar hint of ashes,
   here above the churn,
faint and familiar wood smoke,
sweet earth,
   a garden of flowers turned under,
graceful with symmetry,

swirling like mist,
surrounding this spot on the cape,
memories drifting down the bluff to simply
   dissolve,

returning to the sea, floating away
like the delicate red petals of a rose,

drawn back to our beginnings,
days sitting upon the bench
watching the waves disappear,
melting the horizon into
an endless sunset.

the forever cup

after that first dose
the harsh cocktail of
bitter chemical and poison
there was that thirst

that incredible longing
for the future to be told
the desire for the bottom
to be reached or overcome

filling the cup again and again
hope filled to the brim,
raised and drained once more
a chalice filled with faith
and quiet desperation

all you asked for was
a clean clear glass, with
water perhaps, or warm green tea,
and the luxury of swallowing
in peace, without pain

and yet during the harshest of trials
you gave me a drinking cup,

tall and white, tapered and graceful,
a venti I think it's called

in Italy they raise their cups
arms entwined and touch the rims
the toast is "alla tua salute," and then
they toss it back, ready for another

my cup sits here before me
quietly filled with strong black coffee
elegant and steaming in its silent voice

stamped with the x's
and o's—shorthand for love
and kisses, black letters
on white ceramic

our forever signatures
scrawled on short notes,
some hasty reminders,
or a casual grocery list
where memory might fail

you saw the hope I needed
and the prayers for the sweet taste
of recovery, the slim chance for redemption,
the silent prayers for survival
and perhaps another chance

and so we each drink
from that white cup

etched with the alphabet of forever,
we raise up our cup
"alla tua salute

needing the horizon

yes, we need this balance
we need to see the horizon unfettered,
and the sense of gravity
it affords our unsteady life

sometimes it seems so far off
almost invisible and out of reach,

the hills and treetops hinder our view,
buildings cast their long abandoned
    shadows
obscuring the aim of our vision,

ocean waves surge and roll, dissolving
    vague dividing lines

long straight ribbons of blacktop,
their faded white lines blur the boundaries,
while luring us onward,
towards some journey's end
grasping at a shimmering mirage
and landscapes still out of reach

we are left clutching at a slippery veil of
    echoes

hidden songs of sirens speaking to us,
soft whisperings beyond the pull of
    tides

and at the last glimmer of twilight,
the harsh glare of sunset softens,
affording us a sudden glimpse of
Mercury, the traveler,
    or Zeus on high,

the mysterious green flash
    a sign,
an understanding,

we need
the sight of this horizon to last,
visions of truth,
our purpose here.

three gold bands

my perfect gold band lost one night,
carelessly placed in the pocket of my sweater
hung over a chair during the spirited
    performance,
its weight and warmth secure while my hands
kept a steady rhythm.

I never left that chair until evening's end,
but walking out through the brilliant night
I remember a shiver, a dreamscape, a sudden
    lightness,
and the band was gone.

It was not the first one lost,
yours was flung into the still waters
edging up against the dam. Your
anger and frustration welling up inside,
a rising tide, your heart awash in pain.

cast out into the depths,
out beyond the rocks
your faith and hopes,
confused and desperate,
searching for some firmer ground.

what has become of them?
our hands empty and naked

what has the become of the third band,
that desperate replacement?

was it set aside, concealed
in a keepsake drawer, or
folded in among the
scented remnants
of finer times?

was it tossed aside, without regard,
settled perhaps into a stone cup,
mixed among the buttons and coins of the
     past
the forgotten currency
of promise and fidelity?

I wish I could retrieve them all,
to burnish and buff the surface
of the tarnished precious metals,
restoring them to their
original luster.

could I ever redeem the gold?
could I hold them tightly
in my hands?

I would offer a bond, my vow,
true collateral,
finally recovered and reclaimed,
impervious to all the heartbreak
and the passage of time,

shining proof of our malleable,
but unyielding love.

the white album

I remember the white album
you brought as a gift,
a promise unfolding
in the expectant night.
it was a cold celebration evening,
wrapped and gilded with the warm flush of
   innocence

upstairs in the tiny studio,
we were sheltered inside
so small and intimate a space,
yet so immense in the unseen future

inside the white folded cover,
delightful songs, secrets to be shared
and dark portents of what was to come.
songs, bearing fruit, some bittersweet,
blossomed far past that night,

I still hear those refrains,
dying away, fading into colors
floating above the street,
memories that linger still,
   echoes of white.

swimming upstream

it is now late September
and the water has sufficiently cooled,
fateful sirens have issued their call.

with a furious defiance
these scarlet vestiges school here,
preparing to hurl themselves
through narrow flumes and riffles

exhausted and damaged far beyond instinct
they struggle on, flailing desperately in
one last surge.

they dash themselves against
the cold edges of stone, again and again,
undaunted, bruised and bloodied.

despite their futile efforts
they thrash their way across this landscape
which expects no grace nor
demands any suppleness

sliding for just a brief moment into
shallow eddies, they take a moment's rest
preserved like garnet in startling clear water.

we stand above on the wooden bridge,
its graceful arch laid across this hidden stream,
and watch in silence, transfixed by this tragic
   ballet.

shallow waters etch this agonized passage,
their motion stills
as they escape this realm,
   entering another,

we are privileged, bearing witness to the
   miraculous, divining
the future spawned below.

awash in their own decay,
   transformed,
they gentle settle into vast depths
where instinct for life
endures.

paper sails

that early summer's evening,
winds escaping our grasp,
settling down into the graceful stillness of
    twilight,
warm whispers kissing the delicate green
vines of clematis, the rich sweetness of
    wisteria
swirling like the perfume of youth

as the shadows began to lengthen,
spilling out across the sky,
a soft quilt of darkness gently descends.

there along horizon's edge
a stealthy floating light ascends,
transparent yellow glow of parchment paper,
an angel drifting gently,
its silhouette floating up above the shadows

scraps of golden vellum dance in slow motion,
swirling in a silent ballet, faint parfait of red,
orange, and soft flickering pink,
glowing brighter as the colors melt
finally unfolding into flames,
    ashen lanterns

sails of embers sinking back to earth
their light extinguished, becoming
an ocean of
   dark stars.

tsunami

surrendering to the approaching wave
there is no point turning away,
all will be swept under

a terrible scouring floods the paths,
arriving uninvited into the homes as
well as the hearts of the innocent

the ordinary tides will become a
    torrent
and there is no swell rising slow enough to
    comprehend
the savage aftermath

how can such benign water assault us?
how does the crust and mantle rise up, to
dislodge itself from its slumber
forcing such malevolence upon us?

the innocent now have nothing,
but faith in the rising moon,
the pull of mercy and the opposite motion
    of tides,
the balance of gravity

on the trail

the door flies open and the boys
   head to the trail
marking their secret territories
when feverish abandon overtakes
their casual caution.

muzzles pressing furiously into
every bush and burrow,
scouring for scents
of recent trespasses.

the moist loam is cast out
flung and scattered
into the first light of dawn.

these terriers have not
faltered in their ancient quest

they have not betrayed
their noble lineage.

they return to us so proud
as if to proclaim
   the hunt is on!

time on the road

the two hours or so
it takes to drive to the coast
from this valley,
becomes my meditation.

slick with rain, the road stretches out
like a slender mirror
a shining black pool where
my remembrance floats up,
    lingering,
revealing a clear reflection.

passing by familiar landmarks,
meadows, majestic stands of fir,
and the contours of the riverbed,
I search for something familiar at every turn,
something snatched from memory,
perhaps remade with new vision.

soon, my view expands
beyond this landscape,
and enters new realms.

the horizon is transformed into
a mirage, ancient carvings rebound
off the canyon walls, down to the riverbed.

the road disappears as the light
splinters the smooth seamless stretches,
the ruts and rough patches dissolve,
melting into shadows.

I am not alone in this travelling.
I share this road with others,

like passing sentinels, winding
along this well-worn path.

we exchange the salutes of the day
searching the lanes for comfort,
some wide shoulder where we can stop,
a moment of sweetness savored
and released with a sigh.

soon this part of the journey ends
and the quest begins again,
focusing on the ordinary, oncoming
    traffic.

how often have I inhabited
this familiar road, negotiating
its bends and sharp curves,
cut into the terrain of deer and fox,

an unforgiving black ribbon
trespassing through ancient footpaths
    and riverbeds.

I remember surveying the
slight inclines and steep grades,
thankful I was not climbing them
    alone

but now, I feel compelled to
pull over, abandon my vehicle,
and stride off into the green margins.

leaving the roadbed behind,
embracing the landscape
and start out upon an
unpaved trail.

match hands

we must have been
sitting alone,
a calm moment,
hands clasped together,

perhaps standing in a line,
awaiting entrance,
or admittance—just waiting for
some innocent event
to transpire.

hands joined
in that rare form of intimacy
so absent in
later days.

my father's hands
seemed so large,
hands that were steady
and strong.

hands so powerful
and mysterious,

yet graceful and warm
to a little boy.
the deep mystery of
a depression in the left palm,
a singular flaw
in what seemed perfect

"match hands?"
the boy would ask
and we would press palms together
to assess the difference

stealing a glance, the boy
would linger there
pressing against that left palm
always looking for the mark,
straining to feel the strange stigmata

trying to decipher the mystery
there in the thick flesh,
no larger than a dime,
worn smooth by time and rough labor
that ancient, mysterious,
scar remained

a secret wound
umbilical, healed and
now turned smooth
and pink
around the edges

asking again in their private ritual,
"match hands?"
wanting the pain sealed up

folded inside itself
like silence

"match hands."

bluebird nest

they used to fly everywhere,
here in the meadows and fields of the West
woven into secluded landscapes with abandon,
nesting at the edge of thickets and in the
shadow of ancient oaks, disguised but
    well-tended

they would blend in, unnoticed until spring
when the mother would return,
setting up her cozy abode,
    arranging

the grey nesting bowl just so
tamping down the base and
shoring up the sides for spring and summer,
with sticks and threads, her colorful chattering
    industry

brilliant blue feathers flashing, alert,
in sharp watchful contrast to her grey bower
with constant vigilance and care, patiently
awaiting the return of her mate

and as the mornings warm
with the season, the nests rustle

and faint whispers are heard,
the peeps and chirps
herald a new brood of chicks

they are destined to someday fly away,
some to the cold winds up North
some to the woven plains back East,
others to the warmer, sunny climes
    of the South

filling the air with colorful songs
    hopefully,
returning again to safe nests,
in other spring times,
building rainbow bowers of their own,
    spreading
their precious blue wings,
wending their way home.

innocent house

before leaving we carved a secret niche here
just a small cavity in the structure's bones
a hidden capsule bundled up as if wrapping a
    present,
a secret special treasure,
our time in this house

a picture of then and now,
clippings salvaged from the ashes,
faded to black and white,
a looking back through an unfocused lens

time spent like pieces of forgotten currency,
laid aside for new occupants,
a glimpse at small changes
slowly wrought by days of toil and
    youthful vigor

these walls and windows might whisper of the
    night's passions
betraying the confidence of midnight
and the quiet intimacies of dawn

upstairs, the attic might speak of such
    memories,

crates of letters by candlelight,
set aside to read again

even the warm stone carried in
from the garden, speaks the promise of
    springtime blossoms,
fragrant fruits, and flowers come fall

perhaps the sweet scent of champagne and
    wine will linger
the cork placed here, all relics of ancient
    celebrations
they mark our passage, here and beyond

we give these moments up, a simple offering,
sacraments for unseen occupants
    in days to come
a meager gesture to welcome new lodgers

"welcome home my friends,
share with us this space,
someday you may do the same"

capturing the rituals,
of the past and welcoming
a new future for this innocent
house

round oak table

This old wooden slab,
round oak,
cut and shaped
years ago

a generation beyond my remembrance

you have the rings and
scars of age,
rigors of daily use
lives assembled together

not that you need
to prove anything
beyond
what you are.

you are not damaged goods
in any sense,

despite the
pock markes
and burns.

you are a relic,
a survivor

a victim perhaps,
of casual abuse, or even worse,
utter neglect.

then again,
you are a work of art,
depth and beauty mirrored
in the noble grain
burning and glowing
past midnights,

each scratch
and gouge, polished,
perhaps by tears,

you creak and groan,
revealing lines of age
long-suffering burdens.

bitter sweet sentinels of
winter cold, and the reprise
of warm springs.

you are indeed a sturdy totem,
sixty, seventy seasons and beyond,
who really knows?

in how many rooms
have you stood,
silent and patient,

listening to history
set down before
the family and guests

soaking up secret loves,
spilling out grief and tears

you sit close by the glass pane
our ancient scribe and confessor
looking out, watchful,
beckoning us, to come
closer

gathering one by one,
alone, or all together

let us share our secrets,
bearing our burdens,
our quiet moments,
with you,

our beautiful round oak.

shared space

we live in space, yours and mine
separate but together,
allowing boundaries, like membranes that
protect us, yet yield to insistent pressure

wading in such waters
we share what has drifted before,
moving through what has passed away,
cast off, perhaps returning,
in different forms, fluid shadows
or the steady ripple of stronger currents
    awash in tides

we live in space, alone and
with others, those we may not see
despite our common vision

like a helix, time conjoined, our space
spiraling, a constant distance between us,
a necessary constraint insuring no defect,
protecting this orbit of survival

alone and together we inhabit these spaces,
swallowed up, searching for air,
gasping in the vacuum.

saying I love you

so many times when
we were together, laughing over nothing
or in the silent sharing, a
painful moment, a
private grief divided
   to lighten the load

or when the truth of some simple speech
brought forth your brilliant smile,
so unselfish and radiant,
your brown eyes, glowing, deep and alive,
a penetrating spark, searching and soulful,
exposing my mute thoughts,
   my fears

they dared me to find my voice,
to say out loud words I could
only whisper

holding back the words
"I love you," in spite of my heart

for if I said I love you,
I would be afraid, selfishly,
remaining mute,

longing for you to say it back,
saying I love you
in return.

dust and orchards

the packing sheds still stand,
neglected at the end of long rows
of ancient fig trees, surrounded
by the carcass of sweet fruit withering
on paper trays below

shrouded by zephyrs of dust,
blackened windows are strewn with
the lace of cobwebs, and
desiccated wings of fruit flies
still attempting flight

we would move beneath the dry rustle
    of palm sized leaves, row upon row
dressed in worn khaki and
faded chambray, the sticky white sugars
clinging to our clothes like silk

gathering the fallen issue,
filling paper trays, we marked our slow
    advance
towards the sheds,
sorting the musty fruit by size and condition
cautious in our measuring

the delicate sweetness was
captured within wrinkled skins
the quantity of our currency,
a deep summer bounty
poured into wire baskets and tin buckets,
stained by the rising heat of the morning,

moving through the orchards
the morning glint of sun gives way,
ascending overhead, leading us away from our
    labors
seeking the canopy of shade

the low sweep of misshapen limbs and gnarled
    trunks,
creak under their own weight, older than
    us all
listening to the faint rustle of dry leaves

they speak to us in an ancient language,
gathering us together, taking us away,
leaving room for the others

running away

before I arrived
I knew I would be leaving early,
before the last breath was drawn
and you eased away into a sleep
that would last forever

I wanted to be here with you
during the last most difficult days
to hold your hand and whisper some small
    measure
of love and strength and support,
whispering for me as much as for you

my fear was that you would be gone
before I could arrive, gone too soon--
as if it is ever too soon for death,
ever to soon for a final departure.

and as the days turned longer
your pain eased into your passing
my resolve to stay began to pale, my fearful
shadow slowly fading into grey

even before the service
I saw it descending the slope

away from the gravesite
dissolving before my eyes
melting into tears of regret
floating into the ether of time

the guilt of departure heavy
with each and every step

as the weeks wore on
and your breath softened,
then grew still

I could swear I
heard my footsteps, faint at first,
but louder as I strode away

whispering the words
I could not bear to say

returning

our stretch of rocky cliffs stand
battered by long ocean swells,
swept with the savage winds, and tides,
flooding with the gravity of the moon

harsh waves etch and carve
the deep fissures
    and rifts,
these uplifted stones remain treasured
remnants of past lives,

the rugged shores stand the test of time
daring us to step near, under
windblown mists of froth and foam,
compelling our courage.

we return again and again, like a pulse, a tidal
flow in constant rhythm, filling pools,
those mirrors of the sky.

the smell of the deep sea
    consoles us
ashes blown back to their origins

cast off the crags into the churn below,
her words meld with the Pacific winds
a voice lingering on,
swept up in the graceful mist

a fine shower of prayers and benedictions
"please leave me here, so I may return,
becoming again
    just sand and stone."

where's the moon?

where's the moon?
the young ones cry out,
where's the moon?

the lake water now drawn
down

but at night the reservoir
still seems a swollen sea,
a mirror of stars

and broad pockets of
reeds and cattails
warn of shallows ahead

but this boat still glides
over warm waves before sunset—

and while the evening dims
and grows dark
they scan the sky asking
where's the moon?

the promise of nightfall
sweeps the quiet lake bed

familiar breeze of autumn
wings invisible chevrons
of shorebirds and dusky geese

where is the moon?
these young birds
seem to say

they search the dark-grey horizon
for that precious, promised jewel

impatient youth, yearning
for the passage into night

wide eyes sweep the shore
on lookout for that aurora,
something gleaming yellow,
some celestial diamond

glistening out past the horizon,
skimming over the swell and curl
calming the rolling water

where's the moon
they wail,
where's the moon?

close your eyes young ones
you look too hard

the moon is close by
always there for you,

so reach out until
you can touch it

where's the moon?

take the flowers

I forgot to take the flowers
you offered

how could I?
after all

despite the long show
you were so tired,

worn and burned
by the day's long
talk and excitement

packing up crates of
baskets laden with
your heavy collection of
cards and promises

no use for them,
you said

no use for
these flowers

firmly rooted in
warm soil, close
to the harsh lights,

vibrant with fresh whites,
brilliant yellows and reds.
your flowers stood
in the warm afterglow of
Alderwood, polished myrtle,
with shining copper
rivets

your blue eyes shone in the
offset light, a soft gentle glow
revealing the rigors of days past,

your strong, slender hands,
with that firm grip,
now stained
blood-red

trimming the countless
supple strips of wood

bent and fastened,
sanded tender-smooth

rounded into those baskets,
the ancient artifacts crafted for utility

for a simple purpose,
perhaps to carry flowers
burnished with bright copper rivets
driven straight and true
into stubborn taut corners

they are holding fast to long traditions,
bent wood, carried forwards
with simple, elegant,
grace

I forgot to take the flowers
you offered, but perhaps
you needed them
more than I

those slender green stems,
gleaming in the sharp
corner of your labors

the red and yellow
Inca, the bright orange Poppy, and
Oriental White Lily

yes, I forgot to take the flowers,
but now, I realize
they were designed
to stay with you

a watchful testament,
filling your tiny space, a
sweet and subtle fragrance,
the sweat and oil of alder, mixed
with the stain and varnish of all this
good work

yes,

these flowers belong here,
let them rest with you,
please watch over them

as they will
watch over you

carry them home
when this day is done

place them nearby
let them adorn your
quiet space
they still have much
life to give

cherish them
for what they are

these are your flowers,
you must keep them

a while longer, please,
before you give them
away

storage

drawn to the storage unit
clever closet for the redundant,
vital articles no longer deemed necessary,
shadows of daily life set aside for later,
or perhaps abandoned

still, they issue a call,
as if longing for company or relief,
begging for salvation and comfort,
perhaps absolution from the sins of neglect

the beguiling atmosphere within,
flows through the flux of memory,
   a momentary respite,
remembrances, shrouded in
   dust and cardboard

past life ghosts, hover in silence
winding sheets of leftovers,
forgotten images surrendered,
cast in place like solitary chessmen,
entombed in silent urns
   resting here

hours have passed away,
falling back into memories and faded
    negatives,
grim receipts of passing time

the catalogue of this fragile sanctuary
hovers like a shadow at sunset
waiting for the doors to close

kindred spirit

you must have spent
hours and hours
consulting your ephemeris

the grand mysterious design
a delicate scroll,
systems of script, linkage
and signs

dovetailed like fine joinery, separate
elements fitting together
an eloquent, intricate inlay.

how did you come to this skill?
bent-over the quiet
faraway flame like a candlelit scholar.
a scribe of ancient wisdom
or some sorceress divining
my secret soul with your flickering
    lamp.

how did you foresee all this,
so far in advance
of my knowing?

reading the chart again
after such a long, long time,
I am amazed at this prophecy.

the parchment and tallow
   seal
imprints and insignias still fresh,
thirty-years on,
just now discovering all the road maps
seeking routes to destinations
unknown,

I finally arrive here
at this sacred spot, a locus
now revealed.

how do you know me
better than I know myself?

how could you
divine my spirit
despite my desperate
attempts at disguise?

you were the oracle then,
exotic and forbidden, a
keeper of truths,
secrets held in your heart
sharing yourself with me,

such promises shining through
brilliant brown eyes.
how could you know
all this my
kindred spirit?

how could you have
foretold
these truths?

kindred spirit,
if you still can,

talk to me
now.

long distance

we talked for hours sometimes, our
conversations strung-out well past midnight
and on towards the dawn.

needing not the comforting curtains
of modesty, or the camouflage of whiskey or
    wine,
or the miles and miles of phone lines,
our voices made their tenuous way,
stretching through landscapes far removed.

drawers of scented paper filled with
muted ink, unsent heartbreak
scrawled across yellowed pages
    set aside
tucked long ago inside envelopes
stained and sealed with the salt of regret,
traces of promises unfulfilled.

a thousand words slipping past our lips,
vestige of forever nights, dreams
and sweet whispers
    of your smile

black dog ghost

Sometimes I see him again, here in the early
    morning,
just before the darkness begins to lift its veil
a sudden dash and glint of yellow-green,
his eyes reflected by the sweep and slash of
    headlights
as they arc across the dip and curve of the
    country road,

a futile moment of warning, closing in
on contact, inevitable at such speed,
impulse and instinct not quick enough
to avoid the sickening sound of impact

helpless in one frozen moment,
and then, in a heartbeat, he was gone,
a specter vanishing
into the roadside cover,

back inside the failed camouflage
of dark green shadows,
disappearing like a
    black ghost
evaporating into a shattered sanctuary,
    into stillness.

I have returned this way often, slowing
    as if to make amends
my eyes sweeping the roadside with guilt and
    yearning,
squinting towards the long approach leading
    up to the ranch.

cresting the rise, it becomes a dusty driveway,
children coast down the hill on bikes,
as farmers steer machinery through the
careful geometry of plowed fields.

cattle ensconced safely behind
barbed wire and split poles,
    they bellow and bray,
pressing up against their restraints
yearning for escape.

and sometimes I stop the truck, waiting for the
sharp bark of a black dog.

if I stand frozen and still, silent for a moment,
I believe I see a dark shadow
waiting to cross the road, black tail wagging.

and I swear,
I hear it bark, bark, bark,
sounding a warning to strangers
and all those who dare trespass here.

splendid rendezvous

on the long ride home
through the blackened twists and turns
of the Trinidad highway
I slow, and look for your ghost
alongside the dark roadbed.

I stop and step out, stretching
to stay awake, searching for some sign,
some faint remnant of your presence here,
swirling perhaps along these
furious Klamath rapids.

the midnight air is savage with cold,
shivering, I stop a moment
to look up at the mysterious skies,
brilliantly clear, welcoming me,
an interloper, a stranger.

I have stopped the truck here,
along the grove of huge trees
surrounded by this towering canopy
the constellations of your old haunts

a foolish journey perhaps, yearning
to recover our past inside this dark night
a long sought pilgrimage in vain.

I know this.
you have moved on.

but still I ask of you,

despite the knowing looks and discreet smiles,
they too know you are gone.

the very thought of you here,
long ago,
brings me comfort.

yes, I should have come sooner,
traveling this road
long before,

when your voice still lingered here
singing alongside the river, or perhaps
reading the letters I sent.

I should have listened for those songs.

yes, we could have met here
it would have been
a splendid rendezvous.

burn pile

boards were piled high,
a reckless stack of jack-straws, the
rough-sawn timbers and stout beams
readied for the torch.

yellow streaks of fragrant amber pitch
and sweet sapwood filled the humid
early morning air, ancient forest
chimera of cedar shakes and pine tar
rising from ruin, the ghost of a home.

those boards once stood firm as
walls and floors, sturdy treads rent
from the long staircase, joists and rafters
that once stood strong and proud,
set on the roof's incline, now
collapsed by the indignity of neglect.

these scattered shakes and shingles
kept dry the life within, the simple rooms
    below
sheltered the child's innocent breath,
muffling the climax of lover's moans,
and wrapping the elders safe in
the familiar comforts of a home.

those floors creaked, shifting
under their stately burdens.
windows and doors patiently
settling into the casual
routines of life.

silent footfalls must have crept
along dark hallways, smooth hands caressing
the rails and newel posts, varnish and veneer
polished by breathless moonlight.

set ablaze these planks will burn bright,
the sweet memories engulfed
by white flames, etching
the rich grains into faintly breathing coals,
glowing long past the chill of night

towards the ashes of mourning.

parchment

during the last days, your hands hovered
over the smooth white sheets,
the skin, like gossamer, a delicate
   parchment, the color of pearl,

pale and transparent,
despite the blue veins pulsing,
barely warm along thin wrists, and your
naked, trembling hands,

gold rings and bracelets abandoned
   long ago.

I feel like I am eavesdropping here,
reading a faint calendar, events etched
by broken lines and deliberate scars,
your stubborn stigmata,
   a silent testimony,

your delicate fingers reach out
   towards me,
tracing the furrowed lines on my hands
with the finality of grace,
as if to bid me farewell.

a slight tremor to the touch,
granting me a pardon of flesh
remembering all the caresses and prayers,

savoring the silken filaments of the past,
faint fingerprints of age and involvement.

spreading the clean white sheets
and fine thread count of noble linen,
    tightly wound,

smoothing away the time,
preparing for salvation,
ready for the sweet release of sleep,
and hands finally
at rest.

lingering taste

the white paper birches,
European, canoe, and the
exotic Himalayan,
have all held fast.

their golden leaves shimmer,
well into this crisp
November night.

the graceful sentinels have kept
their brilliant yellow leaves
long past the
big leaf trees.

the majestic oak and stately maple,
butternut and cherry, have long since
surrendered their colors
to the wet landscape
underfoot.

the brisk winds of fall, and
approaching harsh winter, now
stream past.

yet the birches stand
unscathed.

they cling resilient, issuing a
stubborn resolve, exacting the pull
and purpose of crisp,
changing days.

gravity weighs down the tremendous color
of maples and oaks, their
huge, worn patterns, stand defiant,
stark silhouettes etched against
   the autumn sky,

the grace and supple lightness
of birch, the bright white bark
and vibrant yellow leaves resist
the approaching darkness.

the elusive dancers, twist and swirl,
teasing the winds, taunting the elements,
and defy the pressure of rain and wind.

these birch leaves call out to us,
reminding us of the strength
in their gentle swaying motion.

an elegant, lingering, taste
of languishing
summer.

weather vows

after the first ten years together
we were finally ready, finding
ourselves on the storm-crashed crags
overlooking the Pacific Ocean.

last week the view had been immaculate,
spectacular waves of diamonds glittering over
    the water
as far as the eye could see.

but today the cape is cloaked in clouds of salt

wind blown foam
clinging to the deeply carved stones
standing defiant and aloof,

shrouded in spindrift,
hundreds of feet above the rumbling tumult
    below

shorebirds wheeled above us, soaring on the
    updrafts,
disappearing above the fog, their raucous
    calls cast down

perhaps in warning,
a challenge, taunting our
   stubborn endeavor,

floating up on the unseen currents , their
wings outstretched, gliding,
circling, in cloudlike pinwheels
a ballet of ever-widening arcs

were they mocking our insistence and resolve
our refusal to take shelter in the stone hut
perched on the promontory's edge

or heralding our vows
declarations of their own.
their agile freedoms
beckoning us to join them aloft,

freedom dancing , exalting
high up above those crags and pinnacles.

tomorrow the sky would return to blue
and we could see the horizon's breathless
   curve,
miles and miles away,
   out across the faceted sea.

straw hat summer

back home at last, impatient, waiting,
fearful to hear the outcome as
the first results are released.

we have travelled so far to receive the news
that the heat, the liquid gall,
and intrusive scars
have done their work,

fulfilling our hopes, offering
a meager glint of promise

"so far so good," the words are whispered,
and the dream swirls around us, spinning
inside the antiseptic white walls,
an oracle reverberates in our ears,
echo of heartbeats and tremulous sounds
we cannot quite hear.

it was late spring or early summer,
as the calendar speaks, and now,
finally, there was a ray of hope.

recovery would be long,
    achingly slow,

and as the days warmed
prisms of morning dew glimmered
with the chance that you would
    survive.

the sunlight slowly returned to us,
splintered, as if splendid rainbows
herald a return to 'normal,'
whatever that would be.

a miracle, beating such long odds,
a sign you would be coming back,
rejoining life as it was before.

so we sat in the tiny yard,
in that so small a space,
shaded by the young red maple,
its coral red bark
    ablaze
set against the flowering plants
and lush green lawn

a glossy photograph captured your faint
    smile
eyes shaded behind dark glasses,
the loose blue dress,
its summer weight hovering,
angel like, over your skin,
and you wore *that straw summer hat*,
    delicately woven
by some unseen hands,

looking for all the world like
    Turner or Bacall,
poised at their provocative best,
your new straw hat
    tilted back,
gleaming in the sunlight, shining like a
    diamond
discovered in the dark

Authors' Notes

I have always envisioned the process of writing
as a journey, a discovery, uncovering collections
of thoughts, emotions and observations akin to
the gathering of small stones.
Some of these stones were simply cast out,
inspired by the strata of imagination, and some
were chiseled away, carved out of harder rock.

May you hear the music in stones.

About the Author

Raised in the agricultural
richness of the San Joaquin
Valley, William Crutchfield was
born in Memphis, TN and
moved to California as a youth.
He attended California State
University Fresno (1969-1973)
as an English major, and was
greatly influenced by faculty poets, Robert
Mezey, Peter Everwine and Pulitzer Laureate,
Philip Levine. After moving to Eugene, OR,
William graduated with a B.A. in English from
the University of Oregon in 1978 and currently
works in the Willamette Valley as a carpenter.
He cites poets William Carlos Williams, Philip
Levine, Billy Collins, W.S. Merwin and William
Stafford as major influences.